I0697394

Tech Unleashed:

The Apple Foldable Device Chronicles with basic guides

Luca Milne

apple

TABLE OF CONTENTS.....................

Introduction

- About the Book
- The Evolution of Mobile Technology
- Apple's Innovation Journey

Welcome to a deep dive into the uncharted waters of Apple's foray into foldable technology. In this comprehensive exploration, we aim to unravel the mysteries surrounding Apple's potential entry into the foldable device market. From speculations and rumors to in-depth analyses of their innovation journey, this book serves as a guide for tech enthusiasts eager to understand what lies ahead in the realm of foldable devices.

The Evolution of Mobile Technology

To comprehend the significance of Apple's potential leap into foldable technology, it's crucial to trace the evolution of mobile devices. We embark on a journey through the decades, from the brick-sized mobile phones of the 1980s to the sleek and powerful smartphones dominating the market today. The narrative will illuminate the milestones, innovations, and societal impacts that have shaped the landscape of mobile technology.

As technology evolved, so did consumer expectations. The demand for more immersive experiences, larger displays, and increased functionality paved the way for the emergence of foldable devices. We explore the key developments that led to the birth of foldable technology and its evolution from a conceptual idea to tangible products.

Apple's Innovation Journey

Apple, synonymous with groundbreaking innovation, has left an indelible mark on the tech industry. The journey began with the Macintosh in the 1980s, marking the advent of personal computing. The narrative unfolds through the iPod, iPhone, iPad, and Apple Watch eras, showcasing Apple's ability to redefine and revolutionize various product categories.

The book scrutinizes Apple's strategy of entering markets at strategic moments, ensuring their products not only meet but exceed consumer expectations. A meticulous examination of their approach to innovation reveals a company that values quality, user experience, and a commitment to pushing technological boundaries.

Unveiling the Future: Apple's Potential in Foldable Technology

The central focus of this book is Apple's speculated entry into the foldable device arena. As rumors swirl and anticipation builds, we delve into the potential design philosophies, features, and unique aspects that may define Apple's foldable device. By analyzing patent filings, leaks, and industry trends, we aim to provide readers with insights into what Apple's first foldable device might offer.

The book is not only a glimpse into the potential hardware but also a journey into the possible software innovations and integrations that could accompany a foldable device. How would iOS adapt to a foldable form factor, and what novel functionalities might Apple introduce to enhance user experience?

Chapter 1: Unveiling the Future

- The Rise of Foldable Devices
- Apple's Approach to Emerging Technologies
- Speculations and Rumors Surrounding Apple's Foldable Device

The opening chapter immerses readers in the dynamic landscape of foldable devices, tracing their evolution from concept to reality. We delve into the historical roots of foldable technology, exploring the earliest attempts and the technological breakthroughs that paved the way for the emergence of foldable smartphones and tablets. From clamshell designs to the flexible OLED displays that revolutionized the industry, we unravel the narrative of how foldable devices have become a focal point in the ever-evolving world of technology.

Global Adoption and Market Trends

As we explore the rise of foldable devices, we analyze the global adoption trends and market dynamics. Examining the success stories and challenges faced by early entrants, we gain insights into consumer preferences and expectations. From Samsung's Galaxy Z series to Huawei's Mate X, we paint a comprehensive picture of the current foldable device landscape, setting the stage for understanding Apple's potential entry into this transformative market.

Apple's Approach to Emerging Technologies

Historical Innovations

To understand Apple's potential venture into foldable technology, we embark on a journey through their historical approach to emerging technologies. From the introduction of the graphical user interface in the Macintosh to the touchscreen revolution with the iPhone, Apple has consistently redefined user experiences. We examine their innovative ethos, highlighting key moments where Apple embraced new technologies and set industry standards.

Strategic Timing and Market Entry

Apple's reputation for entering markets at strategic moments is a hallmark of their success. This section explores how Apple carefully times its entries into emerging technologies, allowing competitors to navigate initial challenges while Apple refines and perfects its offerings. We analyze past instances, such as the iPod, iPhone, and Apple Watch launches, to draw parallels and contrasts with the potential entry into the foldable device market.

Speculations and Rumors Surrounding Apple's Foldable Device

The Apple Ecosystem Influence

As speculation abounds, we delve into the rumors surrounding Apple's venture into foldable devices. Central to these speculations is the potential integration of a foldable device into the broader Apple ecosystem. How might a foldable device seamlessly interact with other Apple products and services? We explore the possibilities of enhanced continuity and a unified user experience.

Design Philosophies and Features

The chapter delves into the speculated design philosophies and features of Apple's foldable device. From foldable iPhones to iPads, we examine various concepts and leaks that have fueled anticipation. How might Apple address the challenges faced by other foldable devices, such as durability and usability? The exploration includes insights from industry analysts, leaked patent filings, and the tech community's collective imagination.

Market Positioning and Competition

Analyzing the competitive landscape, we discuss how Apple might position its foldable device against existing market offerings. With an emphasis on user experience, ecosystem integration, and Apple's commitment to quality, we explore the potential strategies Apple may employ to carve its niche in the foldable device market.

In Chapter 1, we embark on a journey through the rise of foldable devices, providing a contextual backdrop to Apple's potential entry into this transformative technology. From historical innovations to the intricacies of their approach to emerging technologies, we set the stage for a deeper exploration of the unfolding future in subsequent chapters.

apple

Chapter 2: The Apple Foldable Experience

- The Concept Behind Apple's Foldable Device
- Expected Features and Specifications
- Unique Design Aspects

In this chapter, we delve into the visionary concepts shaping Apple's potential entry into the foldable device market. Unraveling the essence of the Apple Foldable Experience, we explore how Apple envisions blending form and functionality to create a seamless and innovative user interface. From intuitive gestures to interactive displays, we paint a vivid picture of the conceptual foundation underpinning the development of Apple's foldable device.

Enhancing User Interactions

Central to Apple's design philosophy is the enhancement of user interactions. We investigate how the foldable form factor might redefine the user experience, providing not just a larger screen but a transformative way of engaging with digital content. Through an examination of Apple's past design principles and patents related to foldable technology, we decipher the anticipated user-centric features that could set Apple's offering apart in the competitive landscape.

Expected Features and Specifications

Display Technologies

An integral aspect of the Apple Foldable Experience is the display technology. We dissect the potential display technologies that Apple might employ, from advancements in flexible OLED screens to innovative materials that enhance durability and visual clarity. How might Apple optimize the foldable display for vibrant colors, sharp contrasts, and seamless transitions between folded and unfolded states? The exploration aims to demystify the technical aspects driving the visual prowess of Apple's foldable device.

Performance and Processing Power

Examining the expected features, we shift our focus to the performance and processing power that Apple's foldable device might wield. How will Apple leverage its custom-designed processors to ensure optimal performance in a foldable form factor? We analyze potential specifications, drawing parallels with existing Apple devices while considering the unique demands posed by a foldable design. The chapter provides insights into the computational capabilities that users can anticipate.

Camera Innovations

As imaging technology continues to be a key differentiator in the smartphone and tablet markets, we explore the anticipated camera innovations in Apple's foldable device. From advanced sensor technologies to computational photography enhancements, we scrutinize how Apple might elevate the photography and videography experience on a foldable platform. The chapter delves into the integration of camera systems, potential augmented reality (AR) applications, and the role of the foldable design in unlocking new creative possibilities.

Unique Design Aspects

Aesthetics and Build Materials

The aesthetics of Apple's devices have long been a hallmark of their success. We investigate the expected design language, build materials, and finishing touches that will define the exterior of Apple's foldable device. How might Apple balance sleek aesthetics with the durability required for a folding mechanism? The exploration encompasses discussions on material choices, color options, and the overall design philosophy that aligns with Apple's commitment to form and function.

Foldable Mechanism and Durability

One of the critical considerations in a foldable device is the mechanism governing its folding and unfolding. We examine potential foldable mechanisms, drawing from existing foldable devices and Apple's patent filings. Additionally, the chapter addresses concerns surrounding durability, exploring how Apple might engineer a robust solution to withstand the rigors of daily use. From hinge technologies to protective layers, we uncover the intricacies of ensuring longevity in a foldable form factor.

Ecosystem Integration

Integral to the Apple Foldable Experience is the seamless integration of the device into the broader Apple ecosystem. How will the foldable device sync with other Apple products, services, and software? We explore the anticipated ecosystem features that will enhance user convenience, connectivity, and continuity across devices. From AirDrop capabilities to shared workflows, the chapter unveils how Apple aims to create a unified and harmonious experience for users within its ecosystem.

In Chapter 2, we venture into the heart of the Apple Foldable Experience, dissecting the conceptual framework, expected features, and unique design aspects that define this innovative foray into foldable technology. As we explore the blend of aesthetics, functionality, and ecosystem integration, readers gain a comprehensive understanding of what the Apple Foldable Experience might entail.

Chapter 3: The Trend Begins

- Creating a Trend: #AppleFoldableExperience
- Social Media Teasers and Announcements
- Launch Event Highlights

In the digital age, trends often find their genesis on social media platforms, and the anticipation surrounding Apple's foldable device is no exception. This section delves into the strategic creation and promotion of the hashtag #AppleFoldableExperience. We explore the art of crafting a compelling hashtag that encapsulates the excitement, curiosity, and anticipation surrounding Apple's venture into the foldable device arena. From fostering community engagement to creating a unified online conversation, we unveil the strategic use of hashtags as a catalyst for the trending phenomenon.

Encouraging User Participation

A crucial aspect of trend creation is fostering active user participation. We investigate the methods through which Apple and its community can coalesce around the hashtag, encouraging users to share their expectations, speculations, and excitement. From interactive challenges to user-generated content campaigns, we explore how the #AppleFoldableExperience trend can transcend digital boundaries and become a dynamic and inclusive space for Apple enthusiasts worldwide.

Social Media Teasers and Announcements

Crafting Engaging Teaser Campaigns

As anticipation reaches its zenith, Apple strategically releases social media teasers and announcements. This section explores the art of crafting engaging teaser campaigns that captivate audiences and leave them craving more. From cryptic messages to tantalizing visuals, we analyze the components that make an effective teaser campaign, building suspense and generating buzz. By delving into Apple's historical teaser strategies and drawing inspiration from successful campaigns in the tech industry, we unravel the psychology behind creating excitement without revealing too much.

The Role of Influencers and Tech Enthusiasts

Social media influencers and tech enthusiasts play a pivotal role in amplifying the reach of Apple's teasers. We examine how Apple collaborates with influencers to disseminate teasers across platforms. Insights into influencer marketing strategies, teaser reviews, and the impact of influencers on shaping public perception are explored. The section also discusses the delicate balance between maintaining secrecy and leveraging influencers' ability to fuel the anticipation surrounding the #AppleFoldableExperience.

Launch Event Highlights

The Grand Unveiling

The crescendo of the trend is the highly anticipated launch event. This section provides an in-depth exploration of the elements that constitute a memorable and impactful launch event for Apple's foldable device. From venue selection to stage design, we examine the visual and experiential aspects that contribute to the grand unveiling. Furthermore, the chapter delves into the importance of live streaming, global accessibility, and creating an immersive virtual experience for audiences unable to attend physically.

Keynote Address and Product Presentation

An essential component of the launch event is the keynote address, where Apple's key executives take center stage. We analyze the art of delivering a compelling keynote, including effective storytelling, product demonstrations, and strategic messaging. The product presentation section explores how Apple showcases the unique features and selling points of the foldable device, emphasizing the seamless integration into the Apple ecosystem.

Media Reactions and User Feedback

Post-launch, we delve into the media reactions and user feedback that shape the narrative surrounding Apple's foldable device. We explore how Apple navigates the delicate balance between managing expectations and celebrating the achievements of their latest innovation. This section analyzes the role of media reviews, user testimonials, and the immediate impact on market perception, providing insights into the post-launch trajectory of the #AppleFoldableExperience trend.

In Chapter 3, we witness the inception and proliferation of the #AppleFoldableExperience trend, exploring the intricacies of hashtag creation, social media teasers, and the theatrical unveiling during the launch event. As the trend takes on a life of its own, we dissect the key elements that contribute to its success and examine the ripple effects across digital and traditional media platforms.

Chapter 4: Using Your Foldable Device - A Beginner's Guide

- Unboxing and Setting Up
- Understanding the Foldable Interface
- Basic Navigation and Gestures

This section initiates readers into the enchanting world of unboxing Apple's foldable device. We explore the meticulous packaging, unveiling the thoughtfully designed box that houses the much-anticipated device. From the reveal of the foldable device to the accompanying accessories, readers are guided through the sensory experience of unboxing, capturing the essence of Apple's commitment to elegance and precision.

Setting Up Your Foldable Companion

Following the unboxing ceremony, we delve into the essential steps of setting up the foldable device. Readers will be guided through the initial configuration process, from connecting to Wi-Fi to signing in with Apple ID. The chapter demystifies the setup procedure, ensuring a seamless transition for users new to the Apple ecosystem and providing tips for seasoned Apple enthusiasts to optimize their experience.

Understanding the Foldable Interface

Navigating a New Dimension

This section embarks on a journey through the unique foldable interface, unveiling how Apple has reimagined the user experience to harness the full potential of the foldable form factor. We explore the innovative ways in which the interface adapts to both folded and unfolded states, ensuring a fluid and intuitive interaction. From dynamic transitions to adaptive layouts, readers will gain insights into the design principles that make the foldable interface a transformative aspect of the user experience.

App Continuity and Adaptability

A highlight of the foldable interface is its ability to seamlessly transition between different modes. We delve into how Apple has optimized popular applications to take advantage of the foldable display, enhancing both functionality and aesthetics. The chapter explores the concept of app continuity, ensuring that users can effortlessly switch between folded and unfolded states without compromising usability or losing context.

Basic Navigation and Gestures

Mastering the Basics

This section serves as a fundamental guide to navigating the foldable device, introducing readers to the basic gestures that form the cornerstone of the user interface. From swiping and tapping to fold-specific gestures, we provide step-by-step instructions accompanied by visual aids to ensure a smooth and intuitive learning process. The emphasis is on simplicity and efficiency, allowing users to quickly grasp the essential gestures required for daily interactions.

Multitasking in a Foldable World

The foldable form factor opens new avenues for multitasking, and this chapter explores how Apple has integrated innovative multitasking features into the foldable interface. Readers will discover how to effortlessly manage multiple applications, leverage split-screen functionalities, and optimize their workflow in the newfound world of foldable multitasking.

In Chapter 4, readers embark on their journey with the foldable device, from the sensory experience of unboxing to the intricacies of setting up and navigating the innovative foldable interface. This beginner's guide lays the foundation for a seamless and enjoyable user experience, ensuring that users, whether new to Apple or seasoned enthusiasts, can make the most of their foldable companion.

Chapter 5: Advanced Features and Functionality

- Multi-Tasking on a Foldable Screen
- Customization Options
- Enhancing Productivity with Foldable Technology

In this section, readers will delve into the advanced multitasking capabilities of Apple's foldable device. We explore how the expansive foldable screen enables users to effortlessly juggle multiple tasks simultaneously, enhancing productivity and efficiency. From split-screen views to innovative multitasking gestures, readers will discover the myriad ways in which they can optimize their workflow and maximize their multitasking potential on the foldable device.

Seamless App Integration

Central to the foldable multitasking experience is the seamless integration of applications. We guide readers through the process of seamlessly transitioning between apps, leveraging features such as drag-and-drop functionality and app pairing to streamline their multitasking workflow. Through practical examples and step-by-step instructions, readers will gain insights into how they can seamlessly integrate their favorite apps into their multitasking repertoire on the foldable device.

Customization Options

Tailoring the Experience to Your Preferences

This section explores the customization options available on Apple's foldable device, empowering users to tailor their device to suit their unique preferences and workflow. From customizable home screen layouts to personalized app configurations, readers will discover how they can make their foldable device truly their own. We delve into the myriad customization options available, including themes, widgets, and shortcuts, providing readers with the tools they need to create a personalized and immersive user experience.

Advanced Settings and Controls

Beyond surface-level customization, readers will explore the advanced settings and controls that allow them to fine-tune their foldable device to their exact specifications. From display settings to accessibility options, we guide readers through the extensive array of settings available, empowering them to optimize their device for maximum comfort, efficiency, and enjoyment. Whether adjusting display brightness, configuring notification preferences, or customizing input methods, readers will discover how to make their foldable device uniquely theirs.

Enhancing Productivity with Foldable Technology

Redefining Productivity in a Foldable World

This section examines how Apple's foldable device redefines productivity, enabling users to accomplish more in less time. We explore the innovative productivity features and functionalities that leverage the foldable form factor to enhance efficiency and effectiveness. From advanced multitasking capabilities to productivity-focused apps and integrations, readers will discover how they can leverage their foldable device to streamline their workflow, collaborate more effectively, and achieve their productivity goals.

Work and Play in Perfect Harmony

A hallmark of Apple's foldable device is its seamless transition between work and play.

We explore how users can effortlessly switch between productivity tasks and leisure activities, leveraging features such as split-screen gaming and picture-in-picture video playback to seamlessly integrate work and entertainment into their daily routine. Through practical examples and real-world scenarios, readers will gain insights into how they can strike the perfect balance between productivity and leisure on their foldable device.

In Chapter 5, readers embark on a journey into the advanced features and functionalities of Apple's foldable device, exploring the transformative power of multitasking, customization options, and productivity-enhancing features. Through practical guidance and real-world examples, readers will discover how they can unlock the full potential of their foldable device to enhance their productivity, creativity, and enjoyment in both work and play.

Chapter 6: Tips and Tricks

- Maximizing Battery Life
- Troubleshooting Common Issues
- Optimizing Your Foldable Experience

This section is dedicated to empowering users with strategies to extend the battery life of their foldable device. We explore the unique considerations associated with foldable technology and provide practical tips to maximize battery longevity. From optimizing background processes to managing display settings, readers will discover effective strategies for conserving battery power without compromising on functionality. The chapter also covers innovative approaches, such as adaptive power management, to ensure users make the most of their device's battery capacity.

Efficient Charging Practices

In addition to battery optimization, readers will gain insights into efficient charging practices tailored to foldable devices. We explore the impact of different charging methods on battery health and provide guidance on how users can preserve the long-term performance of their device's battery. From understanding optimal charging cycles to leveraging advanced charging settings, readers will learn how to maintain a healthy and long-lasting battery for their foldable device.

Troubleshooting Common Issues

Navigating Challenges with Ease

This section addresses common challenges users may encounter with their foldable device and provides practical troubleshooting solutions. From addressing software glitches to handling hardware-related issues, readers will be equipped with the knowledge to troubleshoot and resolve common problems effectively. The chapter covers step-by-step troubleshooting guides, emphasizing a user-friendly approach to resolving issues and ensuring a seamless and frustration-free experience with the foldable device.

Software Updates and Bug Fixes

Staying up-to-date is crucial for a smooth user experience. We explore the importance of software updates in resolving common issues and enhancing device performance. Readers will understand how to navigate software update settings, implement bug fixes, and leverage the latest firmware to address potential challenges. Proactive maintenance through regular updates becomes a key aspect of ensuring the longevity and optimal functionality of their foldable device.

Optimizing Your Foldable Experience

Tailoring Your Device to Perfection

This section is devoted to providing advanced tips for users to optimize their overall foldable experience. Readers will discover hidden features, shortcuts, and lesser-known settings that can enhance usability and convenience. From gesture-based navigation shortcuts to time-saving automation, the chapter explores how users can customize their foldable device to align with their unique preferences and usage patterns. The focus is on uncovering the full spectrum of possibilities to ensure users extract the maximum value from their device.

Utilizing Foldable-Specific Features

The chapter concludes by highlighting foldable-specific features that distinguish Apple's device in the market. We explore how users can leverage these unique functionalities to enhance their overall experience, from foldable-specific gestures to specialized apps designed to capitalize on the foldable form factor. By understanding and incorporating these features into their daily routine, readers will gain a comprehensive understanding of the nuanced capabilities that make their foldable device truly exceptional.

In Chapter 6, readers are equipped with a toolkit of tips and tricks to navigate the intricacies of their foldable device. From optimizing battery life to troubleshooting common issues and unlocking hidden features, users will gain the knowledge and confidence to tailor their device to perfection, ensuring a seamless and enjoyable experience with Apple's innovative foldable technology.

Chapter 7: Collaborations and Influencer Insights

- Partnering with Tech Influencers
- Unboxing and Review Videos
- User Testimonials and Experiences

This section delves into the strategic art of partnering with tech influencers to amplify the reach and impact of Apple's foldable device. Readers will gain insights into how Apple identifies, collaborates with, and cultivates relationships with influential figures in the tech industry. The chapter explores the symbiotic nature of these partnerships, examining how influencers contribute to building excitement, generating buzz, and shaping public perception around the foldable device. Through case studies and real-world examples, readers will understand the nuances of successful influencer collaborations.

Leveraging Influencer Expertise

In addition to the promotional aspects, this section explores how influencers contribute valuable insights and expertise to the development and refinement of the foldable device. From beta testing programs to collaborative design discussions, readers will discover the collaborative efforts that occur behind the scenes, highlighting the reciprocal relationship between Apple and tech influencers. The chapter also delves into the role of influencers in providing constructive feedback and shaping the ongoing narrative of the #AppleFoldableExperience.

Unboxing and Review Videos

Crafting Compelling Unboxing Experiences

This section unravels the significance of unboxing experiences in the digital age and explores how Apple strategically collaborates with influencers to create compelling unboxing videos. Readers will gain insights into the elements that make an unboxing video memorable, from meticulous attention to detail to storytelling techniques that enhance the overall viewer experience. The chapter also delves into the psychological impact of unboxing videos on consumer perceptions, showcasing how Apple leverages this medium to build anticipation and enhance the overall #AppleFoldableExperience.

In-Depth Reviews and Analysis

Beyond the initial unboxing, this section explores how influencers contribute to the foldable device narrative through in-depth reviews and analyses. Readers will understand the criteria influencers use to evaluate the device, from design and build quality to performance and user experience. The chapter examines how Apple leverages influencers as authentic voices to communicate key features, address potential concerns, and shape the ongoing conversation around the foldable device in the tech community.

User Testimonials and Experiences

Harnessing the Power of User Stories

This section explores the role of user testimonials and experiences in building trust and credibility around Apple's foldable device. Readers will discover how Apple strategically gathers and showcases user stories, highlighting real-world experiences that resonate with a diverse audience. From soliciting testimonials to curating user-generated content, the chapter unveils the mechanisms through which Apple transforms user experiences into powerful narratives that contribute to the overall success of the #AppleFoldableExperience.

Community Engagement and User-Generated Content

The chapter concludes by examining the role of community engagement in fostering a vibrant ecosystem around the foldable device. Readers will gain insights into how Apple encourages user-generated content, from social media challenges to community forums. By showcasing the diversity of user experiences and creating a sense of belonging within the foldable community, Apple establishes a foundation for long-term engagement and advocacy.

In Chapter 7, readers gain a comprehensive understanding of the collaborative efforts between Apple and tech influencers, exploring the impact of unboxing and review videos, as well as the invaluable role of user testimonials and experiences in shaping the narrative around the foldable device. From strategic partnerships to authentic user stories, this chapter unravels the intricate tapestry of collaborations that contribute to the success of the #AppleFoldableExperience.

Chapter 8: User-Generated Content Campaign

- Encouraging User Participation
- Running Contests and Challenges
- Showcasing Community Contributions

This section delves into the strategies employed by Apple to encourage active user participation in the #AppleFoldableExperience campaign. Readers will gain insights into the creation of a vibrant and engaged community centered around the foldable device. From social media engagement to interactive forums, the chapter explores how Apple fosters a sense of belonging among users, encouraging them to share their experiences, insights, and creative contributions within the foldable community.

Call to Action: Sharing Stories and Content

A pivotal aspect of user-generated content campaigns is the effective call to action. This section explores how Apple crafts compelling calls to action, urging users to share their stories, photos, videos, and creative works related to their foldable device. Through real-world examples and case studies, readers will understand the psychological elements that prompt users to actively participate in the campaign, creating a dynamic and ever-evolving tapestry of user-generated content.

Running Contests and Challenges

Gamifying the Experience

This section explores the implementation of contests and challenges as a gamification strategy to elevate user engagement. Readers will gain insights into how Apple designs and executes contests that inspire creativity, innovation, and active participation. The chapter delves into the various types of challenges, from photography contests to app development challenges, showcasing how Apple leverages gamification to make the #AppleFoldableExperience campaign interactive, enjoyable, and rewarding for users.

Prizes and Recognition

An essential component of contests and challenges is the provision of enticing prizes and recognition for outstanding contributions. Readers will understand how Apple strategically selects prizes that align with user interests and preferences, serving as additional motivation for active participation. The chapter also explores the role of recognition in the foldable community, showcasing how Apple acknowledges and celebrates the talents, creativity, and unique contributions of users within the #AppleFoldableExperience campaign.

Showcasing Community Contributions

Creating a Digital Showcase

This section explores how Apple showcases the rich tapestry of user-generated content within a digital showcase, amplifying the voices and talents of the foldable community. Readers will gain insights into the curation process, examining how Apple selects and highlights diverse contributions that represent the global nature of the foldable community. The chapter showcases examples of digital showcases, from online galleries to interactive websites, offering readers a glimpse into the collective creativity and experiences of the #AppleFoldableExperience community.

Amplifying User Stories

Beyond digital showcases, this section delves into how Apple amplifies individual user stories through various channels.

Readers will understand how Apple integrates user testimonials, images, and videos into its marketing materials, creating an authentic and relatable narrative around the foldable device. By giving users a platform to share their stories on a broader scale, Apple humanizes the #AppleFoldableExperience, turning it into a celebration of the diverse and inspiring journeys within the foldable community.

In Chapter 8, readers explore the intricacies of Apple's user-generated content campaign, discovering how the company encourages user participation, runs engaging contests and challenges, and showcases the diverse contributions within the #AppleFoldableExperience community. From fostering a sense of community to amplifying individual stories, this chapter unveils the collaborative and dynamic nature of user-generated content campaigns in the context of Apple's innovative foldable technology.

Chapter 9: Weekly Features and Updates

- Keeping the Audience Informed
- Progress Reports, Leaks, and Official Announcements
- Maintaining Excitement with Regular Content

This section explores Apple's strategy of keeping the audience informed through regular and scheduled updates. Readers will gain insights into how Apple establishes a consistent communication cadence, creating a sense of anticipation and expectation within the foldable community. From weekly newsletters to curated content releases, the chapter examines the mechanisms through which Apple ensures that users stay informed about the latest developments, features, and community highlights related to the foldable device.

Interactive Platforms and Q&A Sessions

To enhance user engagement, Apple leverages interactive platforms and Q&A sessions as part of its weekly features and updates. Readers will understand how Apple fosters a direct and dynamic connection with the foldable community, addressing queries, providing insights, and creating a collaborative space for user interaction. The chapter explores the role of live sessions, forums, and interactive events in maintaining a lively and engaged foldable community.

Progress Reports, Leaks, and Official Announcements

Building Anticipation through Teasers

This section delves into Apple's use of progress reports, leaks, and official announcements to build anticipation and excitement. Readers will gain insights into how Apple strategically releases information about ongoing developments, technological advancements, and potential features of future foldable devices. The chapter explores the delicate balance between controlled leaks and official announcements, examining how Apple leverages anticipation as a powerful tool to maintain buzz around the #AppleFoldableExperience.

Addressing Speculations and Providing Clarity

As part of the weekly features and updates, Apple addresses speculations and provides clarity on various aspects related to the foldable device. Readers will understand how Apple navigates the landscape of rumors and leaks, offering official statements and insights to shape the narrative. The chapter explores the importance of transparency and clear communication in managing user expectations and ensuring that the foldable community remains well-informed.

Maintaining Excitement with Regular Content

Curated Content and Exclusive Sneak Peeks

To maintain excitement, Apple regularly releases curated content and exclusive sneak peeks into the foldable device's features, design, and capabilities. Readers will explore how Apple strategically shares behind-the-scenes glimpses, teaser videos, and hands-on previews to captivate the audience. The chapter delves into the art of storytelling, examining how Apple crafts narratives around the foldable device to create a sustained sense of wonder and anticipation.

User Spotlights and Community Recognition

As part of the weekly features and updates, Apple shines a spotlight on users within the foldable community, recognizing their contributions and experiences. Readers will discover how Apple incorporates user testimonials, creative works, and success stories into its regular content releases. The chapter showcases examples of user spotlights, highlighting the diverse talents, journeys, and perspectives within the #AppleFoldableExperience community.

In Chapter 9, readers explore how Apple maintains a dynamic and engaging relationship with the foldable community through weekly features and updates. From regular communication to progress reports, leaks, and official announcements, this chapter unveils the strategies employed by Apple to keep users informed, build anticipation, and maintain excitement surrounding the innovative #AppleFoldableExperience.

Chapter 10: Countdown to Release

- Starting the Countdown Campaign
- Sharing Daily/Weekly Snippets
- Building Anticipation Leading Up to the Release

This section delves into Apple's initiation of the countdown campaign, signaling the final stages before the official release of the foldable device. Readers will explore the strategic decisions and communications that mark the beginning of the countdown. From teaser events to countdown-specific announcements, the chapter unravels how Apple captivates the foldable community's attention, setting the stage for heightened anticipation and excitement.

Teasing Key Features and Surprises

As part of the countdown campaign, Apple strategically teases key features and surprises that users can expect with the foldable device. Readers will gain insights into how Apple builds intrigue and speculation around specific functionalities, design elements, or unique selling points. The chapter explores the art of controlled revelations, maintaining an air of mystery while providing glimpses into what awaits users upon the official release.

Sharing Daily/Weekly Snippets

Drip-Feeding Information

This section examines Apple's approach to sharing daily or weekly snippets of information during the countdown. Readers will understand how Apple employs a drip-feeding strategy, gradually unveiling aspects of the foldable device to keep the audience engaged. From daily teaser videos to weekly feature highlights, the chapter explores the balance between maintaining suspense and providing valuable insights to ensure a sustained and interactive countdown experience.

User-Generated Countdown Content

As part of the countdown, Apple encourages user-generated content that adds to the excitement. Readers will explore how Apple leverages the creativity of the foldable community, inviting users to share their own countdown content, expectations, and speculations. The chapter showcases examples of user-generated countdown content, highlighting the diverse ways in which users contribute to the collective anticipation surrounding the #AppleFoldableExperience.

Building Anticipation Leading Up to the Release

Interactive Countdown Events

This section explores the organization of interactive countdown events that engage the foldable community leading up to the release. Readers will discover how Apple creates a sense of shared experience, from live Q&A sessions with key figures to interactive challenges and contests. The chapter examines the role of countdown events in fostering a collective countdown experience, building camaraderie among users eagerly awaiting the foldable device.

Exclusive Pre-Order Access and Rewards

To further heighten anticipation, Apple may offer exclusive pre-order access and rewards as part of the countdown campaign. Readers will explore how Apple strategically incorporates incentives for early adopters, creating a sense of privilege and excitement for those participating in the pre-order phase. The chapter delves into the psychology of exclusive access and rewards, exploring how these elements contribute to a sense of belonging and excitement within the foldable community.

In Chapter 10, readers unravel the intricacies of Apple's countdown to the release of the foldable device. From the initiation of the countdown campaign to the sharing of daily/weekly snippets and the organization of interactive events, this chapter unveils the strategies employed by Apple to build anticipation and excitement leading up to the highly anticipated release of the #AppleFoldableExperience.

Chapter 11: The Apple Foldable Community

- Fostering a Sense of Community
- Online Forums and Discussion Groups
- Celebrating the Foldable Enthusiast Community

This section explores how Apple actively fosters a sense of community among foldable device enthusiasts. Readers will gain insights into the strategies employed to create a digital gathering place where users can connect, share experiences, and engage with each other. From dedicated online platforms to community-focused features within Apple's ecosystem, the chapter delves into the intentional steps taken to nurture a vibrant and supportive foldable community.

Facilitating User Interaction

The chapter examines how Apple facilitates user interaction within the foldable community. Readers will understand the importance of features such as comment sections, discussion threads, and user profiles in fostering a dynamic exchange of ideas and experiences. The focus is on creating a space where users feel comfortable expressing their thoughts, asking questions, and forming connections with fellow enthusiasts who share a passion for the #AppleFoldableExperience.

Online Forums and Discussion Groups

Curating Engaging Discussion Spaces

This section explores the role of online forums and discussion groups in the Apple foldable community. Readers will gain insights into how Apple curates engaging discussion spaces where users can explore topics ranging from technical troubleshooting to creative use cases. The chapter delves into the structure and design of these forums, examining the features that contribute to a user-friendly and collaborative environment conducive to meaningful interactions.

Expert Moderation and Support

The chapter also highlights the importance of expert moderation and support within online forums and discussion groups. Readers will understand how Apple ensures that these platforms are not only spaces for discussion but also hubs of valuable assistance and guidance. Through the presence of knowledgeable moderators and support teams, users can receive timely help, fostering a culture of mutual aid and shared expertise within the foldable community.

Celebrating the Foldable Enthusiast Community

Spotlighting User Contributions

This section explores how Apple celebrates the diverse talents and contributions of the foldable enthusiast community. Readers will discover how Apple spotlights user-generated content, success stories, and creative works, creating a space where users feel acknowledged and appreciated. The chapter showcases examples of community spotlights, illustrating the varied and inspiring ways in which users contribute to the collective narrative of the #AppleFoldableExperience.

Exclusive Community Events and Perks

The chapter concludes by examining how Apple organizes exclusive community events and provides perks to celebrate the foldable enthusiast community. Readers will gain insights into how these events serve as opportunities for users to connect, share insights, and participate in unique experiences. Whether through virtual meetups, exclusive product previews, or community-specific perks, Apple reinforces a sense of belonging and appreciation among foldable enthusiasts.

In Chapter 11, readers explore the intentional efforts made by Apple to foster and celebrate the Apple Foldable Community. From creating digital gathering places to curating engaging discussion spaces and spotlighting user contributions, this chapter unveils the strategies employed to nurture a vibrant, supportive, and celebrated foldable enthusiast community around the innovative #AppleFoldableExperience.

Conclusion

- Reflecting on the Journey
- The Impact of Apple's Foldable Device
- Looking Towards the Future

As we conclude this exploration into Apple's foray into the foldable device market, it's essential to reflect on the journey we've undertaken. From the early speculations to the unveiling of features, the countdown to release, and the vibrant community that has emerged, the narrative surrounding the #AppleFoldableExperience has been a dynamic and captivating journey.

Readers have delved into the meticulous strategies employed by Apple to introduce, market, and engage users with its innovative foldable device. The journey has not only been about the technology itself but also about the community that has formed around it—a community fueled by anticipation, creativity, and a shared passion for pushing the boundaries of mobile technology.

The Impact of Apple's Foldable Device

The impact of Apple's entry into the foldable device market is profound, transcending the realm of technology. The foldable device has not only redefined user interactions and experiences but has also influenced the broader landscape of mobile innovation. Through strategic partnerships, influencer collaborations, and a robust user-generated content campaign, Apple has succeeded in creating a cultural phenomenon with the #AppleFoldableExperience.

From a technological standpoint, the foldable device has pushed the boundaries of what users can expect from their mobile devices. The unique design, advanced features, and seamless user interface have set new benchmarks for the industry. Apple's meticulous approach, characterized by a careful review of emerging technologies and a commitment to delivering a product that aligns with its standards, reflects the company's dedication to providing users with transformative and reliable experiences.

Looking Towards the Future

As we conclude this journey, it's natural to turn our gaze towards the future. The foldable device market is still in its early stages, and Apple's entry has undoubtedly sparked a new wave of innovation and competition. How will other tech giants respond? What further advancements can we expect in foldable technology? These questions linger as we anticipate the continued evolution of mobile devices.

Moreover, the foldable community that has formed around the #AppleFoldableExperience is poised to play an integral role in shaping the future narrative. As users continue to share their stories, insights, and creative contributions, the community becomes a driving force in influencing how the technology is perceived and utilized.

In conclusion, the #AppleFoldableExperience is not just about a device; it's about a collective journey, a community-driven exploration into the possibilities of foldable technology. As Apple continues to innovate and users continue to engage, the future promises exciting developments and a continued evolution of the mobile landscape. The foldable journey is ongoing, and the pages of this narrative are still being written, shaped by the ever-evolving intersection of technology and community.